Bay of Fundy's Hopewell Rocks

BAY OF FUNDY'S
HOPEWELL ROCKS

KEVIN SNAIR

GOOSE LANE

Cover and page design by Kevin Snair with Julie Scriver.
Cover photograph by Kevin Snair.
Printed in China by MCRL Overseas Printing.
10 9 8 7 6 5 4 3 2 1

Goose Lane Editions acknowledges the generous support of the Government of Canada, the Canada Council for the Arts, and the Government of New Brunswick.

Goose Lane Editions is located on the unceded territory of the Wəlastəkwiyik whose ancestors along with the Mi'kmaq and Peskotomuhkati Nations signed Peace and Friendship Treaties with the British Crown in the 1700s.

Goose Lane Editions
500 Beaverbrook Court, Suite 330
Fredericton, New Brunswick
CANADA E3B 5X4
gooselane.com

Library and Archives Canada Cataloguing in Publication

Title: Bay of Fundy's Hopewell Rocks / Kevin Snair.
Names: Snair, Kevin, author, photographer.
Description: Previously published: Riverview, New Brunswick: Chocolate River Publishing, 2015. | Includes index.
Identifiers: Canadiana 20220493812 | ISBN 9781773103211 (softcover)
Subjects: LCSH: Hopewell Rocks (N.B.) | LCSH: Hopewell Rocks (N.B.)—Description and travel. | LCSH: Hopewell Rocks (N.B.)—Pictorial works. | LCSH: Hopewell Rocks (N.B.)—Guidebooks. | LCSH: Rocks—Fundy, Bay of. | LCGFT: Guidebooks.
Classification: LCC QE446.N49 S63 2023 | DDC 552.09163/45—dc23

The author and the publisher have made every effort to ensure that the information contained in this guide is as accurate as possible. Over time trails may change for a variety of reasons. Trail maintenance, improvement, or relocation may make this guide inaccurate in places. Although the author indicates some of the potential hazards on some of the trails, neither the author nor the publisher accept any liability, implied or otherwise, for accident, loss, injury, inconvenience, or any other damage that may be sustained by anyone using the information contained in this book. Those who rely on the information contained herein do so at their own risk.

For Laura, the love of my life and source of endless encouragement

Aerial view of the Hopewell Rocks

CONTENTS

Sun dog over Big Cove

PROLOGUE

The following is an excerpt from Moncton's
The Daily Times, dated August 27, 1892

The next morning we visited the famed rocks. Originally the place must have been a high bluff composed of conglomerate or pudding stone. Through the action of the waves for countless ages, the place has been converted into the most weird imposing character imaginable. An American gentleman who recently visited this locality says that he has cruised in every nook and corner of the coast of this country but none could compare in grandeur with these rocks. By the incessant action of the waves, caverns have been cut into the rock formations, some to quite a length. In places the waves have left huge boulders, standing erect like grim sentinels, which rise up sphinx like in their loneliness, some with tufts of vegetation growing on their tops. Speaking of sphinxes, one of these is shaped marvelously like one of the seven wonders, it only requiring a little use of the chisel to convert the rough work into a veritable statue.

Residents bemoan the fate of what were called *the twins*, two figures that stood out in bold relief quite near the shore and which looked remarkably like two female figures, the head, bust, waist and drapery being very lifelike. Some of the caverns are of quite a depth, one in particular having a history. Its hidden depths have not yet been fully explored, the timid ones being informed that it is impossible to reach the innermost recesses, mysterious noises being heard and unseen hands of waves snuffing out artificial lights. The indentations run along the cliffs for perhaps 200 yards and every year the merciless waves cut further into the vitals of its charming enemy.

The scene at the rocks during a heavy blow must be an interesting one. With a heavy sea on, the waves, mountains high and driven with a swish into the caverns and against the perpendicular walls, only to fall back, beaten like a cur must indeed be a sight terrific in its sublimity.

A BRIEF HISTORY

Glooscap

THE MI'KMAQ

THE MI'KMAQ PEOPLE saw the Hopewell Rocks as a special place and favoured it for ceremonies and gatherings.

The Mi'kmaq People have a number of Traditional Stories relating to the Rocks and the tides of the Bay of Fundy. This is one that the late Michael Francis heard from his grandfather who heard it from his father.*

> For hundreds, perhaps thousands of years before the arrival of the Europeans, the very powerful, very wise men of the Mi'kmaq people would gather together annually during the fall natural harvest. These men were called Ginaps. They would travel to the place of their "cooking pots" guided to the location by six-foot-high carved poles (waa geige). Mi'kmaq men, women, and children travelled long distances to come together for feasting, dancing, singing, and spiritual ceremonies. Food for all the people was provided by the Ginaps, who would prepare everything that was needed in their large cooking pots.
>
> This annual gathering was carried on for centuries until the European missionaries arrived. They convinced the people to take down the carved guiding-poles, saying that their enemies from the west would surely find them if the poles remained standing. With the pulling out of the sign poles and with the dying off of the Ginaps, the gatherings at the cooking pots ceased. The big pots themselves turned to stone. We can still see them today as the Hopewell Rocks or flowerpots. The Rocks have remained in Mi'kmaq memory as a special place to go to meditate and to pray, especially if there was a shortage of food among the people.

*Reprinted with permission from: Allen, Patricia, Michael Nicholas, and Fidèle Thériault. 2004. *Rocks Provincial Park: The 1994 Archaeological Survey and Historical Inventory*. Fredericton: Archaeological Services, Heritage Branch Culture and Sport Secretariat.

DesBarres map of 1777 depicting the Merry Dancers

Remainder of a breakwater on North Beach

EUROPEAN SETTLEMENT

THE 1600S SAW the arrival of the first European settlers in the area. History tells us that French explorers named the area Cap Demoiselle because of the similarities between the picturesque rocks and their fine "young maidens" back home. Colonel Joseph DesBarres expanded on the comparison in his famous atlas, *Atlantic Neptune*, referring to the Rocks as *Merry Dancers*.

The French Acadians built dykes to keep the giant tides off the salt marshes, allowing them to farm these otherwise unusable lands. Remains of these dykes can still be found at the north and south ends of the park. The English resettled the lands after the Acadians were deported in the mid-1700s. In the late-1800s, landowners erected breakwaters to preserve the dykes, which were slowly being destroyed by the constant beating of the tides.

Our first known sketch of the Hopewell Rocks was published in 1840 by Abraham Gesner, New Brunswick's first provincial geologist. In his geological survey, he explained, "In other instances, the united powers of the tide and waves wear out rude caverns, and with uncouth sculpture, form isolated blocks, which at a distance resemble the work of art."

Abraham Gesner sketch circa 1840

Rocks excursion circa 1900

In the late 1800s and early 1900s, the Rocks become a favourite venue for Sunday school picnics, family drives and other outings.

When owners Charles and Claudine Ayer built a restaurant and dance hall on the lower site in 1926, the Rocks started to become a park. The Rocks Pavilion, as it was called, became well-known for weekend dances. I once asked one local resident if she would perchance have any photographs of her times spent at these dances. A sly smile worked its way across her face as she told me, "Oh, my dear, we wouldn't want any pictures of what went on there."

Prime Minister R.B. Bennett

ON JULY 24, 1928, five to six thousand people assembled at the Park grounds over-looking Hopewell Rocks to hear soon-to-be Prime Minister R.B. Bennett give his first Maritime speech as Leader of the Opposition. Bennett shared his memories of growing up in the area and addressed the importance of finding a way to harness Fundy's tidal power for energy.

Members of the New Brunswick Gas & Oilfield Limited at the Hopewell Rocks circa 1930

Exploring the Rocks circa 1900

Heading down the staircase circa 1934

IN THE LATE 1920S, a large wooden staircase was built in what is now known as Staircase Cove. To my knowledge, this was the first set of stairs built on the site, and visitors could now use these stairs to access the ocean floor instead of relying on North Beach or Demoiselle Beach.

The Park's popularity grew with both travellers and locals. In the summertime, children would rush to finish their chores so that they could go swimming in the creek where the Ayers had constructed a swimming hole. In the winter, the same area was used for ice-skating. A section of the frozen pond was marked off-limits because the Ayers would cut large blocks of ice from it and move them to a nearby ice house. The blocks would be packed in sawdust and stored until summer when they would be used to create ice cream.

The Rocks Pavilion circa 1937

Memories of the swimming hole by John Jones

THE AYERS built rental cabins by the pavilion. One rental resulted in tragedy for Mrs. Reesa Mitchell in the summer of 1947.

On July 1st, 1947, a recently widowed man named Ginn rented a cabin for himself and his five children while his newly purchased home in Gunningsville was being made ready. The next evening he rented a second cabin for his housekeeper, Mrs. Reesa Mitchell, so she could help look after the children.

Ginn later confessed to the police that he and Mrs. Mitchell left the cabin around 3 p.m. on July 5th and headed to a clearing in the woods. Both had been drinking and they carried their liquor-laced pop bottles with them. They had a history of arguing, and this time an argument broke out over $50. Ginn claimed that Mrs. Mitchell insulted him by saying his children were not his and she threw her bottle at him. He saw it coming and ducked. Then he struck her with his bottle, which he said, "knocked her out and I moved her a few feet into the woods." He covered the body with leaves.

The following day, Ginn packed up his children and took them to his in-laws' home in Bay Verte before he went to the RCMP in Moncton and confessed to everything. He took the officers to the scene of the crime, pointed out the body, and said, "Now do you believe me?"

Ginn went on trial for murder in Hopewell Cape and was found guilty of manslaughter seventy days after the crime was committed. The all-male jury chose manslaughter over murder after agreeing that "no man could be expected to allow such an insult…especially if he had been drinking." He was given a four-year sentence and incarcerated in Dorchester prison. Although today we would find the verdict a great injustice against women, it tells us a lot about the male-dominated society of the 1940s.

Since Reesa Mitchell's death in 1947, a number of people have reported seeing the ghostly figure of a lady at the head of the Rocks Road. Could she be haunting the Hopewell Rocks?

One of the rental cabins in the 1930s

Playing in Big Cove circa 1935

New staircase circa 1957

THE AYER FAMILY never charged admission to the park, but they did have a donation box on the main stairway. Herbert Ayer inherited the park from his parents and continued to operate it with his wife Bea (Myrtle Beatrice Palmer) until the province expropriated it in 1958. One item of note is that a very professional staircase was built in behind **the *Mother-in-Law*** rock a few years prior to the expropriation. I can't help but speculate that the government assisted in the building of those stairs and that this was perhaps a foreshadowing of things to come.

Under provincial ownership, the park has seen many changes. The 1960s saw the Rocks Pavilion replaced by a new restaurant and gift shop. Many new souvenirs were created to help guests remember their visit. The cabins were sold, and tenting sites were created. Hazel Trites, a long-standing employee of the park, wrote a fascinating six-page book called A Story of The Rocks and sold it for 25¢ per copy. One can feel her passion for the park as she wrote, "One should also see The Rocks on a moon-light night when the tide is high and viewed from above the shore. The water running through and among the rocks appears to be molten gold."

Three more expropriations (two in 1988 and one in 1995) and one purchase in 2019 led to the resulting 275-acre park as we now know it. In 1998, the New Brunswick government contracted the management of the park to Serco, an international company. Under their vision, the park underwent its largest renovation to date. They built the massive parking lot at the upper site; an Interpretive Centre with scientific displays, a gift shop, restaurant, and reception area; and a café at the lower site. They also built over three kilometres (two miles) of trails to connect the upper and lower sites and Demoiselle Beach and furnished them with lookout decks so visitors could see the Bay at both high and low tide. Serco continued to manage the park until 2006 when they moved out of the recreation and leisure field internationally.

In 2007, Hopewell Rocks officially became a park under the Provincial Parks Act. Each year, over a quarter million visitors travel from all corners of the earth to experience the wonder of the Bay of Fundy tides at the Hopewell Rocks.

Souvenirs and postcards from the Hopewell Rocks

FUNDY'S GIANT TIDES

Tide simulation

THE BAY OF FUNDY has the highest tides in the world. If you really want to experience the difference between high and low tide, try kayaking over the area that you explored on foot just a few hours earlier.

Low tide 0 metres (0 feet)

At the Hopewell Rocks, high tides range from 10 metres (32 feet) to 14 metres (46 feet) in height. The timing of high tide varies by about fifty-two minutes per day because the earth has to rotate more than one full rotation to realign with the ever-elusive moon.

High tide 14 metres (46 feet) approximately 6 1/4 hours later

Tide coming in at North Beach

TWO MAJOR FACTORS give the Bay of Fundy the largest tides in the world. The first is the fact that the bay is shaped like a giant funnel. As the moon and sun pull the water into the narrowing bay, the water is forced into a tighter and shallower area. There is nowhere for the water to go, so it rises.

The other factor is the length of the bay. The Bay of Fundy is just the right length for the tide to enter the bay, go all the way to Moncton and return in about twelve hours and twenty-six minutes. This means that just as one tide is exiting the bay, the next one is trying to come in. The two collide and amplify one another. Scientists call this resonance the *seiche* effect, or the bathtub effect, because the water is sloshing back and forth like the water in a bathtub.

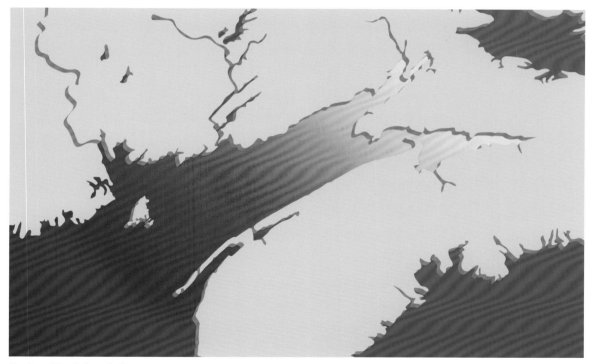

The Bay of Fundy funnel effect

Moonrise over the Bay of Fundy

A QUICK GLANCE at a tide table will show visitors that not all tides are the same height. These differences in height may seem random, but they are actually very reliable. The variation in height is influenced by factors such as the phase of the moon, time of year, and distance between the moon and the earth. Just as the planet paths are predictable, so are the tides. Tides are extremely complicated, so here is a very simplified explanation.

The moon has the largest influence on the earth's tide. On average, the moon is only 384,000 km (238,600 mi) from earth, which allows the moon's gravitational pull to draw the ocean water up toward it. As the earth rotates, this bulging ocean water continues to be attracted to the moon, causing a wave or tide of water that is aligned with the moon. Due to the combined movement of the earth and moon, we also get an equally large bulge of water on the opposite side of the earth at the same time. At any given time, there are two high tides and two corresponding low tides on earth. They are called lunar tides because they are influenced by the moon. As the earth rotates, these lunar tides ebb and flow at the Hopewell Rocks.

Lunar Tides

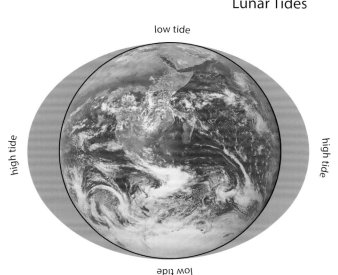

low tide

high tide

high tide

low tide

Moon

THE SUN has a similar pull on the earth's waters, but the effect is much weaker. At approximately 149,000,000 km (98,500,000 mi), the sun is much further away from the earth. These tides are called solar tides.

Solar Tide

The way the sun and the moon interact to influence the world's oceans also accounts for some of the height variation in the tide table. When the sun, moon and earth are in alignment during the new or full moons, the lunar and solar tides work together and augment one another, producing an extreme tide known as a spring tide, even though the name has nothing to do with the season. Guests who wish to see tides at their best should plan to visit around the full or new moons when both the lunar and solar high tides are aligned. This is when they will see the highest high tides and lowest low tides; the difference between them can reach over 14 metres (46 feet).

Spring Tide

Seven days later, the moon has orbited a quarter of the way around the earth putting it at a right angle to the sun. At this point, the effects of the sun's gravitational pull are working against those of the moon. Instead of co-operating, the solar tide now robs water from the lunar tide. We still get a high tide on the part of the earth that is closest to the moon, as well as one on the opposite side of the earth, but these tides are smaller and called neap tides. Neap tides can be as little as 10 metres (32 feet) at Hopewell Rocks. It is worth noting that along with lower high tides, we also experience higher low tides at Hopewell Rocks during this phase.

One other factor that affects the daily height is the position of the earth and moon in their elliptical orbits. When the moon is closest to the earth, and the earth closest to the sun, their pulls on the tides are greatest.

Neap Tide

Moon

high neap tide

low neap tide

low neap tide

high neap tide

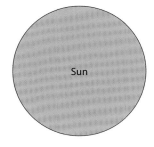

Sun

Tʜᴇ sᴛᴀғғ ᴀᴛ ᴛʜᴇ Hᴏᴘᴇᴡᴇʟʟ Rᴏᴄᴋs are constantly searching for new ways to help their guests understand the tides. On August 13, 2014, three interpretive guides (Ryan, Meagan and I) conducted a demonstration during one of the highest tides of the season. We anchored our feet and allowed the tide to rise around us. To the amazement of onlookers, it took a mere 27 minutes for the tide to rise from our feet to Meagan's chin.

Start: We strapped the weights to our feet and awaited the oncoming tide. A crowd of just over one hundred people gathered nearby to watch the spectacle.

8 minutes: The tide was already to our knees. Although the water was cold, we were sure we could tolerate it for the duration of the demonstration.

15 minutes: *The water was now waist deep. Large fish were bumping against my shins and nibbling at Meagan's toes. The sediment in the water made identifying the fish impossible.*

21 minutes: *As the tide reached mid-chest, it became harder to ignore the chill. We finished eating our pizza (delivered by kayak) and reaffirmed our resolve to remain till the end.*

27 minutes: *You could see the unease growing on Meagan's face as the tide slowly enveloped us. Once it reached Meagan's chin, we slipped out of the weights and walked to shore.*

THE ROCK FORMATIONS

Midtide in Castle Cove

Exploring North Beach

HOW THE ROCKS TOOK FORM

THE STORY OF THE BIRTH OF THE HOPEWELL ROCKS begins over 330 million years ago and features some of nature's most powerful forces that have been battling since the beginning of time. Eon after eon, storms rained down on the nearby Caledonia Mountain Range and washed small rocks and sediment into the level valley below. Millions of years passed, and this sediment got higher and heavier, pressing on the layers below. Eventually this pressure transformed the layers into a unique type of rock that is now known as the Hopewell conglomerate.

After this, nature treated the area to some major tectonic action as the continents repositioned themselves. The resulting pressure thrust these rocks upward at a 30–40 degree angle, which you can see in the photo to the left. This also caused vertical fractures that segmented the rock until it resembled a tightly packed jigsaw puzzle.

Then, a mere 13,000 years ago, the last of this region's great glaciers melted. As they melted, the weight on the land lessened. The land rebounded and then settled into its present position about 6,000 years ago. The water released from the glaciers formed rivers and streams that flowed into the Atlantic Ocean. Ocean levels rose and allowed salt water to break over the ancient land mass between Massachusetts and Nova Scotia that is now known as George's Bank. The ocean spilled into the valley between what is now Nova Scotia and New Brunswick/Maine, creating the Bay of Fundy with its giant tides.

Those tides battered against the Rocks twice a day, and the soft conglomerate rock started to erode faster. The vertical fractures widened and separated the jigsaw-like pieces. Some pieces crumbled into the sea, and others were left as the free-standing formations we see today.

THERE ARE many erosive forces or agents that continue to attack the Rocks today. Some agents, such as wind and rain, work on the entire rock. Other agents, like the tide and floating ice, work only on the lower parts that can be reached by the rising water.

The two photographs below show that little erosion has taken place on the upper part of *The Sentinel* rock formation over the last seventy years. However, the lower third has battled the tides twice daily over that time period and has narrowed considerably. Experts use comparative photos like these to predict how much longer a formation like this may last.

At the Hopewell Rocks, the greatest annual erosion happens in the spring when the cracks of the Rocks are exposed to a daily freeze/thaw cycle. It's tempting to view erosion as a negative force that is destroying the Rocks, but it's important to remember that it was erosion that first started carving the formations out of the conglomerate cliffs 6,000 years ago.

The Sentinel in Castle Cove in the 1940s   *The Sentinel in Castle Cove circa 2010*

Remnants of rock fall in 2011

THE ROCK FORMATIONS

Visitors have been naming the rock formations ever since they started coming here. Some of the earliest names were **Man's Head** and **The Sentinel**.

This postcard featuring **Man's Head** was created circa 1904. Unfortunately, he lost his head somewhere around 1915.

The remainder has slowly been eroding away and is no taller than his visitors today. Here is the same scene in 2014.

No one is quite sure when *Mother-in-Law* first got her name, but she has been a guest favourite for decades. Other visitors think she also resembles a pharaoh or even George Washington.

E.T. from North Beach (above) and ***Anteater Rock*** from Cut-Off Cove (below) are hard to miss once you know what you are looking for.

Dinosaur Rock in Staircase Cove (above) and ***Baby Elephant*** from Cut-Off Cove (below) in their natural and imagined states

THE INTERTIDAL ZONE

Seaweed covered rocks at low tide

The intertidal zone is found on the shoreline between the high and low tide marks. It is a fascinating place to explore. Because the area is under water for part of the time and exposed to the air at other times, it hosts an ecosystem that is found nowhere else. The intertidal creatures found here also need to be able to tolerate the reddish brown sediment that is suspended in the water. The Bay of Fundy has the highest tides in the world, so Hopewell Rocks has one of the largest intertidal zones.

Guests sometimes wonder where all the sea creatures are, but you can find them if you know where to look.

Family exploring in Staircase Cove

Hermit crab (Paguroidea)

Sarah L holding the squid eggs she found on the ocean floor

Anemone

WHEN THE TIDE STARTS TO RECEDE, try inspecting the plant life on the rocks. Many types of seaweed grow on the rocks within the park, and knotted wrack and bladder wrack are abundant. Knotted wrack is a long plant with air bubbles spaced along its length. Visitors see it lying flat on the rock, but when the tide comes in these bubbles help the plant float close to the surface. The bladder wrack is flatter and has pods that tend to be mitten shaped and filled with algin (a thickening agent used in the production of ice cream, tooth paste, and numerous skin-care products). If you comb through the seaweed, you may find periwinkles, barnacles, and even the occasional crab.

Barnacles

Knotted wrack (Ascophyllum nodosum)

Bladder wrack (Fucus vesiculosus)

As the tide continues to drop, more beach is uncovered. Occasionally, one can find squid eggs, finger sponges, and fish that have been left behind by the tides. The most commonly stranded fish are long-finned squid, followed by small tommy cod, monkfish, and even skate. Hornwrack can be found blowing along the beach like tumbleweeds. Although it looks like a plant and is even named wrack, if you look closely you will discover it is actually a colony of tiny animals. Mermaid's purses are another favourite beach find. These are the egg sacks of skates or sharks and are often found caught in the seaweed at the high tide mark.

Long-finned squid (Loligo pealei)

Hornwrack (Flustra foliacea)

Mermaid's purse

As the tide reaches its lowest point, guests may have to venture as far as 200 metres (220 yards) to reach the water's edge. The shoreline here is muddier, but the creatures are more plentiful. Small tide pools host a variety of dog whelks and hermit crabs. Both Atlantic rock crab and the smaller green crab can be found skittering along the rocky shoreline. The mud supports sea snails, worms, and mud shrimp, which in turn become food for the shorebirds. If you are fortunate enough to be visiting during a spring low tide, when Hopewell Rocks experiences its lowest low tides, a beautiful assortment of sea anemones may become exposed on the rocks before the tide quickly covers them again.

Atlantic rock crab (Cancer irroratus)

Anemone

Sea lettuce

Hermit crab (Paguroidea)

Waved whelk

Semipalmated sandpiper (Calidris pusilla)

THE BAY OF FUNDY is also an important feeding ground for the semipalmated sandpiper. Up to 95 percent of the world population of these birds stop here on their migration south. This can result in numbers upward of one hundred thousand at a time between mid-July and late August. The sandpipers feed on mud shrimp (*Corophium volutator*), and biofilm to double their weight so they can fly non-stop to South America. It's a seventy-two-hour flight; if they don't fatten up here, they may not make it.

Peregrine falcon (Falco peregrinus) watching for sandpipers

Highly magnified mud shrimp (Corophium volutator)

Semipalmated sandpiper (Calidris pusilla)

Bald eagle (Haliaeetus leucocephalus)

Birds of prey are common in the Park as well. Bald eagles can often be seen soaring overhead as they search for an easy meal. There are at least four bald eagle nests within ten kilometres of the Park.

PEREGRINE FALCONS were almost extinct in Atlantic Canada until they were reintroduced in the mid-1980s. These birds can reach speeds of up to 390 kilometres per hour (240 miles per hour) when they are diving, making them the fastest creatures on earth. They have nested above Big Cove since 2009, and many visitors have been thrilled to catch a glimpse of the nest from the comfort of Big Cove lookout. Raising young peregrines is challenging work for the parents. Although three or four eggs are commonly laid, success of the brood has varied from years when four fledge successfully to years when none survive.

Peregrine falcon (Falco peregrinus) and young

SEASONS OF THE PARK

Jupiter Rising over Cut Off Cove

Original flowerpot near sunset

Fiddlehead

SPRING

S PRING IS ALL ABOUt new life in the park. Birds make their nests, wildflowers emerge from their winter sleep, and the promise of new beginnings is in the air.

Park staff get busy patrolling the trails, cleaning them up from the winter, and preparing them for the season ahead. Experts are brought in to examine all the formations and cliffs for changes in stability and to remove loose rubble that could endanger guests.

Rock scaler inspecting the cliffs

Young great horned owl

Baby American redstarts

Strolling through Castle Cove

Sunrise at Lover's Arch

SUMMER

SUMMER IS FULL of life and activity at the Hopewell Rocks. Guests visit from all over the world, drawn by the raw beauty of the rock formations and sheer power of the tides.

The shore birds start arriving in late July and can outnumber the human visitors by fifty to one. Their synchronized flight on their daily journey to Mary's Point and back has often been compared to a ballet over the water.

Sunny afternoon in Big Cove

Sandpipers landing on North Beach

Blueberries

Garter snake

Rock balances on Demoiselle Beach

Peeking into Big Cove

Fireweed

Groundhog

AUTUMN

Autumn nights get cooler and the number of visitors declines, but the ones who are brave enough to stick around are rewarded with nature's most spectacular show. The colours of the Bay of Fundy come alive in late September when the leaves on the hardwood trees turn a mixture of yellows, oranges, fiery reds, and deep crimson.

Many of the birds begin to head south for the winter, leaving the Hopewell Rocks in peaceful solitude.

E.T. stands alone

Maple leaves in full brilliance

Sunset over Daniels Flats

WINTER

T HE HOPEWELL ROCKS take on a whole new feeling in the winter. The park is closed due to the added risks of slippery ice, falling icicles, and unmarked danger zones. Here is a behind-the-scenes look at the park at this dangerous time of year.

Looking through Lover's Arch

The Sentinel in winter

The Bay never fully freezes because of the constant movement of the water, which can also deposit large chunks of ice on the shoreline. It is easy to assume the tides simply come in and go out; but, in reality, the tides flow in a complex pattern of surface currents that are best observed by tracking the floating ice.

Runoff from above freezes and forms large icicles on the underside of the rock formations. These icicles can reach lengths of over three metres (ten feet) and can look like giant swords suspended from the overhanging cliffs above.

Icicles at North Beach   *Red squirrel warming in the winter sun*

Giant icicles

E.T. under snow

A frozen Cut-Off Cove

The Milky Way over Lover's Arch

NIGHT

A T NIGHT, the beach is stripped of all sense of time. Every sound echoes off the cliff faces. The Milky Way silhouettes these stone giants and makes you feel like you are one of the first explorers who were guided here by the stars. You can feel very small in this wondrous place.

Observing the night skies

A rare glimpse of the northern lights from North Beach

Darkness adds another level of danger to the park. Tripping hazards are harder to avoid, and there are no lights on the paths, trails, or shoreline. The rocks have a primitive feel like you just walked onto a movie set for a new version of *The Land That Time Forgot*.

Staircase Cove under starlight

Next Page: Exploring Staircase Cove

SELF-GUIDED TOUR

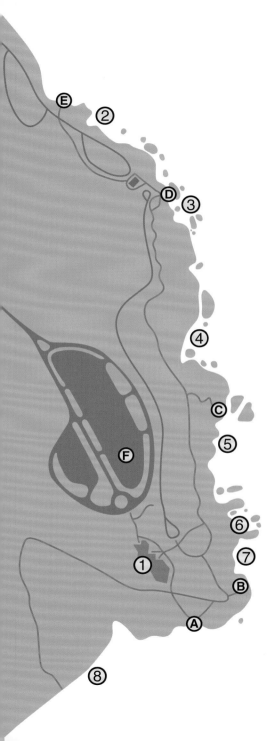

1) **Interpretive Centre:** Interpretive displays, gift shop, washrooms, restaurant

2) **North Beach:** Original Flowerpot Rock, Mother-in-Law, E.T.

3) **Staircase Cove:** Dinosaur Rock, Lover's Arch, Bear Rock

4) **Castle Cove:** Castle Rock, Apple Rock, the Sentinels

5) **Big Cove:** Elephant Rock, Sea Cave, Mattress Rock

6) **Cut-Off Cove:** Anteater Rock, Baby Elephant, Glooscap

7) **Diamond Cove:** Diamond Rock, Emergency Platform, the ledges

8) **Demoiselle Beach:** Double Eye of the Needle, the mudflats

A) **Daniels Flats lookout**

B) **Diamond Cove lookout**

C) **Big Cove lookout**

D) **Main Deck**

E) **Stairs to North Beach**

F) **Parking Lot**

SELF-GUIDED TOUR

THE HOPEWELL ROCKS PARK offers a variety of opportunities to connect with nature, ranging from quiet forest paths to sea caves and open beaches. The amount of mud on the ocean floor can vary from non-existent to unavoidable depending on the prevailing winds and how far you choose to venture at low tide. Rubber boots or hiking boots are recommended, but a quick stop at one of the convenient boot-wash stations can erase a multitude of missteps. Always pay attention to the tide times and heed the warnings of park guides.

This tour starts at the Interpretive Centre. If the tide is coming in, you may want to rush down the trail to the staircases at either Main Deck or North Beach because you can visit the lookouts at any time, but you can only access the ocean floor at low tide.

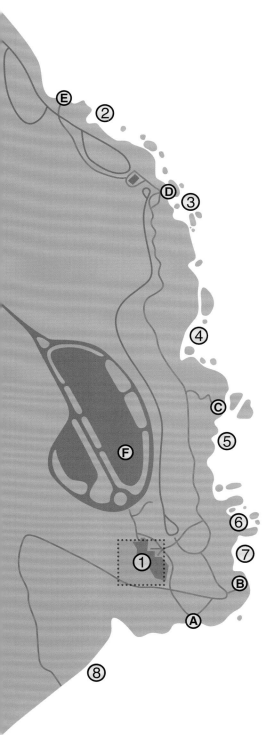

1. INTERPRETIVE CENTRE

THE INTERPRETIVE CENTRE serves many purposes. Within its walls you will find a full-service restaurant, a well-stocked gift shop, and the main information area. Many informative displays explain the science of the tides, geology of the Rocks, and the delicate ecosystem of the Bay of Fundy. No visit would be complete without touching the giant whale's tail, which is made to feel like the skin of the endangered Atlantic right whale.

Outside the Interpretive Centre are the pathways that lead to the lower site and the four lookouts (Daniels Flats lookout, Diamond Cove lookout, Big Cove lookout, and Main Deck). A trail directly behind the Centre will take you on a delightful stroll down to Demoiselle Beach. For those who are unable to walk the trails or choose not to, a shuttle service is available between the upper and lower sites for a nominal fee.

Displays in the Interpretive Centre

A. DANIELS FLATS LOOKOUT

Daniels Flats lookout is located directly behind the Interpretive Centre. It provides an amazing overview of the expansive mud flats that are revealed as the tide recedes. Over the centuries, Demoiselle Creek has cut a permanent snake-like path through the ever-changing mud. You can just imagine Samuel de Champlain's consternation when, according to legend, the receding tide left his ship high and dry here in the early 1600s.

View from Daniels Flats lookout at high tide

View from Daniels Flats lookout at low tide

B. DIAMOND COVE LOOKOUT

D IAMOND COVE LOOKOUT is only a short walk from the playground and provides spectacular views of both Diamond Rock and Daniels Flats. To the north, the passage under Diamond Rock fills with water at high tide, restricting access to all but those fortunate enough to have a kayak. To the south, you can see Grindstone Island ten kilometres away. Grindstone Island separates Fundy's waters from the rich muds of the estuary.

High tide

Low tide

C. BIG COVE LOOKOUT

If you continue along the main trail towards the lower site, about halfway down, you will find a side trail that leads to Big Cove lookout. It is one of the lesser-used decks in the park, but the view is definitely worth the walk. Not only can you look over the full expanse of Big Cove, you may also get a rare peek into a nest of the once-endangered peregrine falcon.

Low tide

High tide

D. MAIN DECK

Tʜᴇ ᴠɪᴇᴡ ꜰʀᴏᴍ Mᴀɪɴ Dᴇᴄᴋ is probably the most photographed vista in New Bruns-wick. It is the best place to view high tide, and, if you look down on the familiar *Lover's Arch* formation, you can see for yourself the change in water height over a very short period of time. At low tide you can access the ocean floor via the stairs that lead down to Staircase Cove or you can continue to North Beach, which offers a wheel-chair-grade ramp. If the tide is high, you can grab a quick coffee or snack at the Low Tide Café.

Evening high tide from Main Deck

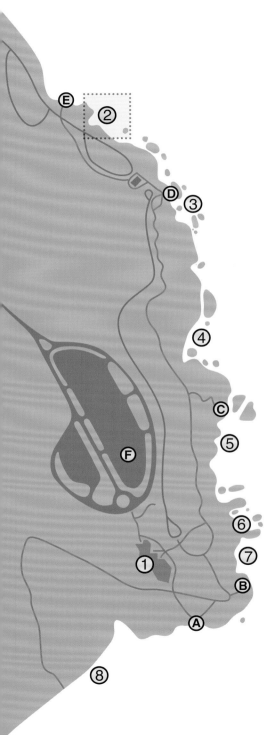

2. NORTH BEACH

NORTH BEACH provides the easiest access to the ocean floor because it offers a gentle ramp as opposed to the stairs of Staircase Cove. The hike of Hopewell Park's shoreline is approximately 1.8 kilometres (1 mile) and it can only be attempted at low tide. If you look to the north, you can view the vast mudflats where the sandpipers feed. Around mid-July, you may start to see them huddled on the beach here at high tide.

As you head south, you will encounter the *Original Flowerpot Rock* and then the *Mother-in-Law*. Around the next corner, you come face-to-face with *E.T.,* which was called *The Sentinel* in the early 1900s.

After you venture around the next outcropping of rocks, you will find yourself in Staircase Cove.

Ramp at North Beach

Looking toward North Beach

Original Flowerpot Rock

Mother-in-Law

E.T.

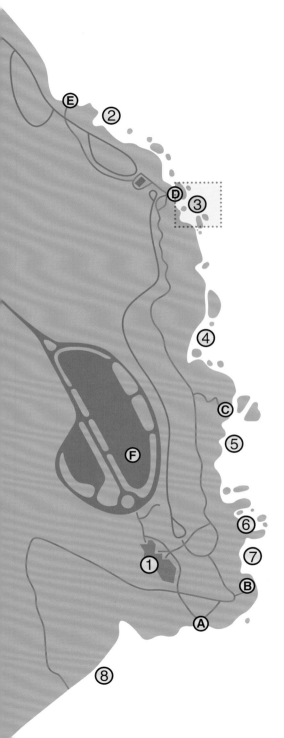

3. STAIRCASE COVE

WHETHER YOU ENTER from North Beach or come down the staircase from Main Deck, Staircase Cove is a must see for any visitor to the park. If you are short on time or about to be caught by the incoming tide, you may only have time to explore this cove. But this cove boasts some of the most famous rock formations, so it will not disappoint you.

In the middle of the cove stands *Lover's Arch*. Many claim it is named because it looks like two faces kissing, but the name could simply refer to the fact that the two rocks lean on one another for support as lovers often do. The archway is a favourite place to have a souvenir photo taken and has even served as a spectacular location for a number of weddings over the years.

Just to the south of *Lover's Arch* is *Bear Rock*; named because it resembles a large black bear sitting on its hind legs and gazing up into the woods. *Bear Rock* was attached to *Lover's Arch* until the late 1970s when a large section of rock collapsed and separated them forever. *Dinosaur Rock* to the north is a favourite with both the young and young at heart.

Staircase built in 2016

Lover's Arch

Dinosaur Rock

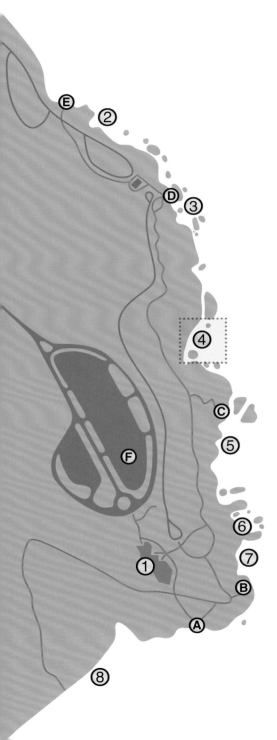

4. CASTLE COVE

Castle Cove is one of the mid-sized coves in the park. The cove is named for the large formation on its north end that used to resemble a castle. Known as *The Devil's Cave* in the early years, *The Castle* was a favourite to explore until Sept 26, 2002 when a couple hundred tons of rock collapsed before the eyes of onlookers. This made *The Castle* unsafe for the public to enter and it remains cordoned off to this day.

Just outside *The Castle* entrance, you can find *Apple Rock*. This is a remnant from another rock fall that happened over half a century ago. It sat upright until the winter of 2011, when it cracked and shifted off its base. As tempting as it looks, climbing is not permitted, again for safety reasons.

On the south end of the cove stand the *Three Sentinels* that guard *The Castle*. The main sentinel may be one of the next formations to fall, but just behind it is a great example of a new flowerpot being born. In the decades to come it will likely become free-standing because it is only attached to the mainland by two small pieces which can be seen in the photo on the opposite page.

Looking south in Castle Cove

Looking north in Castle Cove

This formation will become free standing as this erodes.

Apple Rock

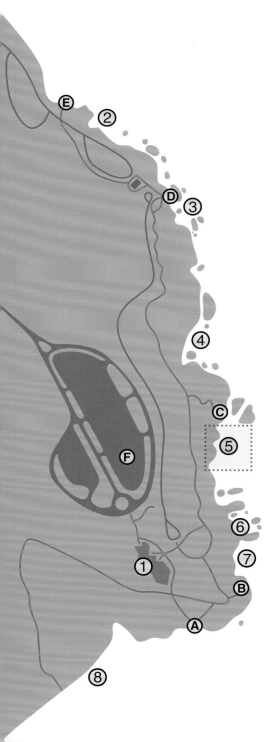

5. BIG COVE

Big Cove is named for its great size. You can reach it from Castle Cove through a passageway on the right-hand side of *Elephant Rock*, which lost its trunk to calving in 1997. *Elephant Rock* suffered further injury in the spring of 2016, when an additional calving event dislodged hundreds of tonnes of debris. The debris was deposited between *Elephant Rock* and the *Sea Cave.*

You can also take a passageway near the water that leads you to the opening of the *Sea Cave*, one of the hidden gems of the park. If you venture up the 45 degree slope to the top of the cave, you can stand at eye level with the high tide mark. This is arguably the best place in the park to appreciate the volume of water that enters the bay twice a day. When you are done in the cave, you can return back down the slope and continue around the shoreline to Big Cove.

In the middle of the cove, you may notice a large flat rock that looks oddly out of place. *Mattress Rock* is believed to have floated into the cove when it was embedded in ice back in the 1930s. It is a favourite surface for spreading out a family picnic.

If you are lucky, you may also spot one of the once-endangered peregrine falcons that have nested in the cliffs of this cove since 2009.

View from inside Sea Cave

Looking north in Big Cove

Elephant Rock in 2013

Elephant Rock after calving in 2016

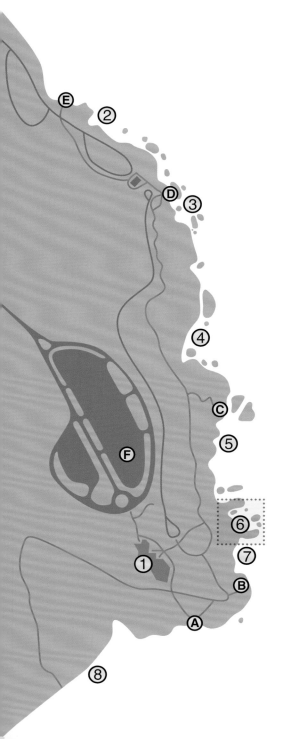

6. CUT-OFF COVE

Cut-Off Cove received its name because it is the first point of land to be covered by the sea. If you don't pay attention to the incoming tide, you will find yourself cut off from the way back. Fortunately this is not a concern during park hours as staff are posted here at critical times to ensure that all visitors are safely off the beach before they can be stranded by the tide.

This is one of the smaller coves, but it has a number of interesting rock formations. As you enter from Big Cove, you will come face to face with *Anteater Rock* and *Baby Elephant* just up behind him on the right. The tall formation in the middle of the cove resembles a face from this vantage point and is referred to as *Glooscap*.

To continue on, you can exit this cove by going along the water's edge, which is often muddy, or go through a tunnel under *Diamond Rock*.

Wide view of Cut-Off Cove

Anteater Rock

Baby Elephant

Glooscap

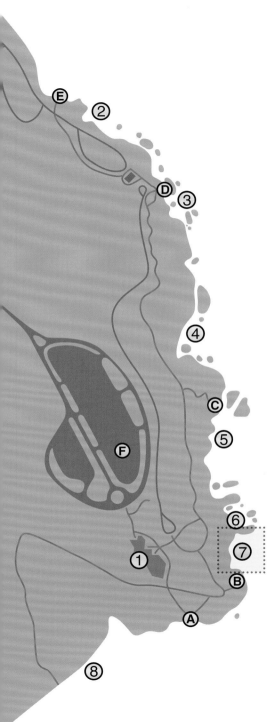

7. DIAMOND COVE

IF YOU CHOSE TO ENTER DIAMOND COVE through the tunnel, the first thing you will see is a large tower in the distance. This emergency tower is not an exit, but it will provide a safe place to wait if you find yourself stranded by the tide. It is intended for emergency use only and may not be climbed for any non-emergency use.

The south end of Diamond Cove is bounded by a large outcropping of rocks that extend all the way to the water's edge. They are referred to as the ledges and are made up of many large, slippery boulders overlapping at precarious angles. These rocks are different from those found in the rest of the park and are primarily a calcite limestone. The ledges contain amazing examples of fossilized algae called *stromatolytes*. These *stromatolytes* are evidence of an ancient seabed dating back over a billion years, and the algae's photosynthesis was a key contributor to the creation of today's atmosphere.

Progressing over the ledges is not recommended without proper footwear because the boulders become treacherous when wet. For this reason, most visitors will turn around at Diamond Cove and head back to either the stairs at Staircase Cove or the ramp at North Beach. Turning around also gives you a great view of **Diamond Rock**, the diamond-shaped rock above the tunnel that leads back to Cut-Off Cove.

Emergency tower in Diamond Cove

Stromatolytes

Diamond Rock

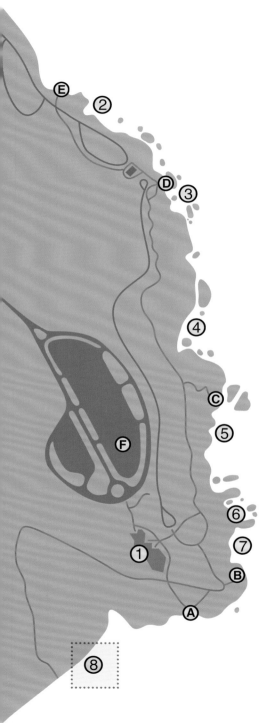

8. DEMOISELLE BEACH

DEMOISELLE BEACH, on the other side of the ledges, is one of the hidden gems of The Rocks. This beach is not easily accessed from the other coves so it is often overlooked. However, you can take the 1.2 km trail that starts behind the Interpretive Centre. The shaded trail is lined with informational panels and ends at a large beach. At low tide, the mudflat extends as far as the eye can see, but the mud is out of bounds to visitors because of the mud shrimp that make their home in its rich sediment. This is another place where you may see the sandpiper flocks. If you do, please don't disturb them because they need to fatten up.

Many guests and the occasional staff member enjoy the ancient pastime of rock stacking at the northern end of the cove where there are many rocks of various shapes and sizes. Sometimes you can come across whole villages of rock people and other constructions that appear to defy gravity just waiting for the tide to come in and reduce them back to rubble.

This is the only beach in the park where the view of sunset isn't blocked by the high cliffs. The setting sun paints the rocks a beautiful rosy brown as the day comes to a close.

View from the southern border of the Park

Rock balance on Demoiselle Beach

Double eye of the needle as seen when approaching from over the Ledges

ACKNOWLEDGEMENTS

Tɦɪs ʙᴏᴏᴋ would not have been possible without the help of many. I would like to thank the people of Albert County. When I first started gathering the history of the park, you opened your homes, memories, and family photo albums to me and I am forever thankful.

I wish to thank all the staff and management at the Hopewell Rocks. You have all been so supportive of my undertakings and have inspired me to learn more and more about the park. Beyond the help you have extended to me, I want to thank you for the enthusiasm with which you greet our guests, cook and serve their food, prepare souvenirs, clean the floors, cut the lawns, guide tours, answer questions, shuttle our guests, and generally make visiting the Hopewell Rocks a world-class experience.

I would like to thank my family for your endless encouragement and sacrifices as I spent more and more time in the park and away from you. Without your support, I would never have dared to spread my wings and attempt an undertaking such as this.

PHOTO CREDITS

All photographs, illustrations and diagrams by Kevin Snair with the following exceptions:

p. ix: Moncton Museum Collection

p. 4 top: Map reproduction courtesy of the Norman B. Leventhal Map Center at the Boston Public Library

p. 5: Image courtesy of Canadiana Collection (http://canadiana.library.ualberta.ca/index.html), a digital initiative of the University of Alberta Libraries

p. 6: Steeves House Museum

p. 8–9: Moncton Museum Collection

p. 10 top: Steeves House Museum; bottom – Vaughn Snider Photo Collection

p. 11 top: Barbara Ayer Ricker Photo Collection; bottom – painting by John Jones

p. 13 top: Sharon Steeves Postcard Collection; bottom left – The family of Vivian Stiles; bottom right – Ruth Young Photo Collection

p. 16–17: photo by Kevin Snair courtesy of The Hopewell Rocks

p. 18: photo by Kevin Snair courtesy of The Hopewell Rocks

p. 19: photo by Kevin Snair courtesy of The Hopewell Rocks

p. 81 left: Chocolate River Publishing

To see more of Kevin Snair's photography and videos, visit www.creativeimagery.ca.

INDEX

Page numbers in **bold** denote illustrative material.